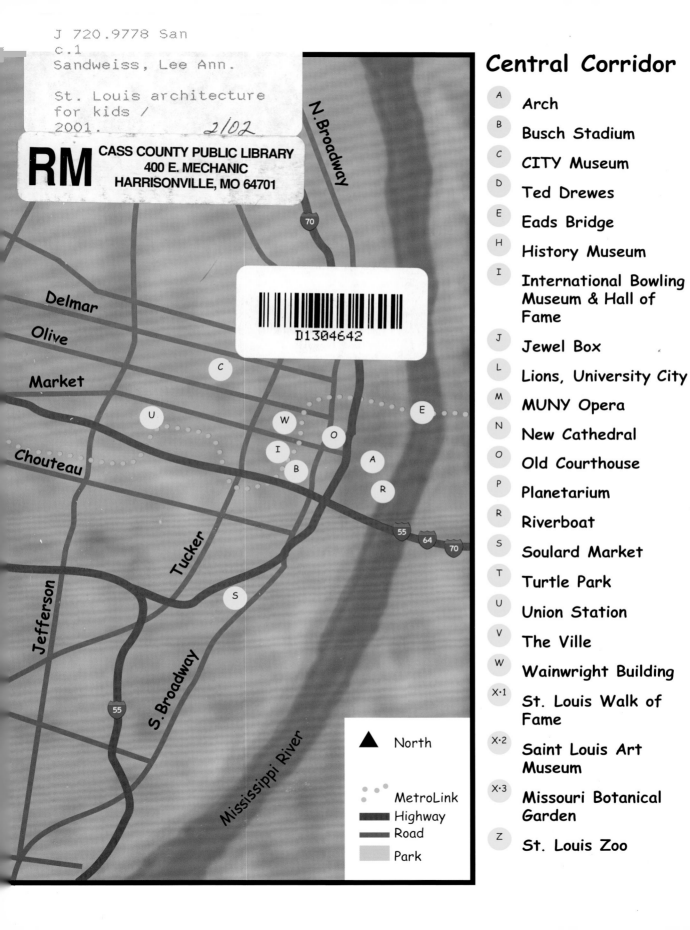

Central Corridor

- **A** Arch
- **B** Busch Stadium
- **C** CITY Museum
- **D** Ted Drewes
- **E** Eads Bridge
- **H** History Museum
- **I** International Bowling Museum & Hall of Fame
- **J** Jewel Box
- **L** Lions, University City
- **M** MUNY Opera
- **N** New Cathedral
- **O** Old Courthouse
- **P** Planetarium
- **R** Riverboat
- **S** Soulard Market
- **T** Turtle Park
- **U** Union Station
- **V** The Ville
- **W** Wainwright Building
- **X·1** St. Louis Walk of Fame
- **X·2** Saint Louis Art Museum
- **X·3** Missouri Botanical Garden
- **Z** St. Louis Zoo

North

MetroLink
Highway
Road
Park

ST. LOUIS ARCHITECTURE for KIDS

By Lee Ann Sandweiss
Illustrated by Phyllis Harris
Photography by Gen Obata

Missouri Historical Society Press
Saint Louis

By the Mississippi, in the heart of this land,
There's a river city that truly is grand.
My name's Archy. Come along with me—
I'll show you St. Louis, from **A-to-Z**!

To show that St. Louis is the start of the West,
The Gateway Arch towers above all the rest.
Admired by millions for its strength and its grace,
The **Arch** marks St. Louis as a most special place.

Busch Stadium, we know, holds quite a crowd.
When the Cardinals are winning, it's certainly loud!
Loyal fans wear red to all the home games.
They cheer with a bird—and Fred is his name.

B

On Washington Avenue, where factories once were,
There's **CITY Museum**, which caused quite a stir.
A zany place built out of found odds & ends,
A warehouse of fun, made for you & your friends.

C

A hot day in St. Louis is just not complete
Without a stop at **Ted Drewes** for tasty concrete.
This thick frozen custard's the talk of the town—
It stays in the cup when it's turned upside down!

Built long ago in 1874,
The **Eads Bridge** stretches to the Illinois shore.
More than a mile of wrought iron and steel,
This beautiful structure still has great appeal.

E

Faust Park is the home of an old carousel,
That once in the Forest Park Highlands did dwell.
Up and down its fine horses merrily prance.
The calliope music makes them all dance!

F

No place in St. Louis has quite the charm
Of the historic site known as **Grant's Farm**.
Feed the baby goats, see the Clydesdales roam—
It's open to all, this President's home!

G

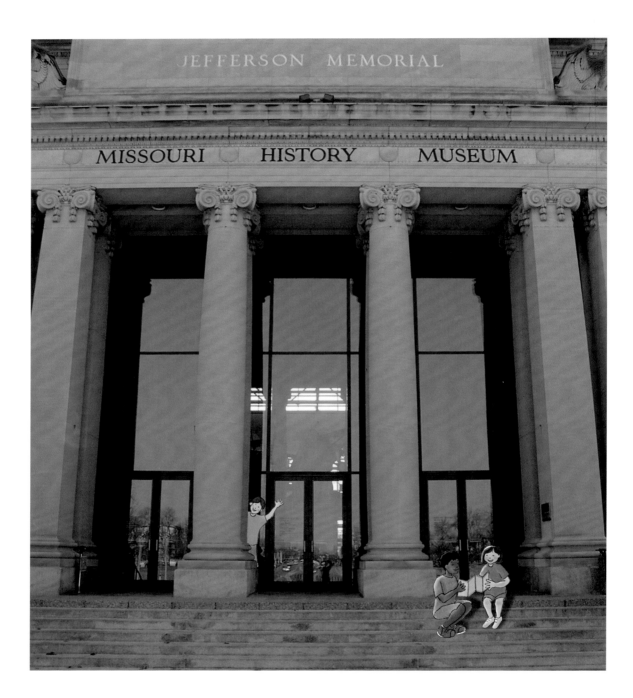

Missouri History Museum shares many stories
About St. Louis's past, its people, and glories.
Learn about Lindbergh or the splendid World's Fair.
If you're seeking St. Louis, you'll find it all there!

The **International Bowling Museum and Hall of Fame**
Tells the 5,000-year history of this popular game.
See the bowling pin car—a wacky contraption,
Or bowl on real lanes for a taste of the action.

I

Forest Park has a precious **Jewel Box**
That holds fragrant treasure and seldom is locked.
A building of glass where lovely flowers grow—
In winter, it looks like a gem in the snow.

J

If travel by train sets your heart aglow,
To **Kirkwood Depot** you might go.
A limestone station down by the tracks
That can take you to Kansas City and back.

K

Lions are the most regal of beasts—
Sometimes found where expected the least.
High upon pillars they stand proud and tall
And guard the entrance to U. City Hall.

At the **MUNY** on a warm summer night,
The gigantic stage is flooded with light.
There's a crowd of 10,000 and more coming in.
Better hurry up, folks—the show's about to begin!

M

The **New Cathedral**'s mosaic interior
Is known through the world as simply superior.
You are welcome to go there and linger awhile
To admire this masterpiece fashioned in tile.

The **Old Courthouse** has a magnificent dome,
A local landmark many pigeons call home.
Long ago some thought, "This building's not practical!"
Yet it was a model for our nation's Capitol!

St. Louis has a hyperboloid
That lets you gaze out into the void—
The **Planetarium** is just the place
To study the stars in vast outer space!

P

In winter there's a swell place to skate.
In summer the Pops series is great.
It's got a museum where the exhibits bark!
This fun-filled place is **Queeny Park**.

Q

A **Riverboat** ride means old-fashioned fun.
Take a stroll on the deck when the day is done.
Nothing's as pretty and nothing's as fine
As a fiery sunset behind the city skyline!

If fresh fruit or flowers are your target,
You must visit **Soulard Market**.
The farmers' bounty is certainly ample.
If you ask them politely, they'll give you a sample.

S

Near Highway-40 is a curious sight—
Huge concrete turtles give children delight.
Boys and girls climb and play until dark
At a playground we call **Turtle Park**.

Trains once came here from Detroit to Dallas,
To stop at this building that looks like a palace.
If downtown St. Louis is your destination,
Be sure that you visit our grand **Union Station.**

U

The **Ville** is a neighborhood filled with pride
And Sumner High School is one reason why.
Artists, athletes, politicians of fame
Are sons and daughters that Sumner can claim.

V

In downtown on North 7th Street,
Stands an architectural feat.
The **Wainwright Building** is known through our land,
Designed by Louis Sullivan's hand.

St. Louis Walk of Fame

Saint Louis Art Museum

Cahokia Mounds

Ready for more? Your adventure's not done!
Visit these places for **X-tra** fun!

X

Museum of Transportation

Laumeier Sculpture Park

Missouri
Botanical
Garden

X

y

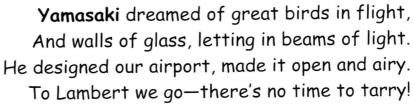

Yamasaki dreamed of great birds in flight,
And walls of glass, letting in beams of light.
He designed our airport, made it open and airy.
To Lambert we go—there's no time to tarry!

Our world famous **Zoo** within Forest Park
Has more animals than old Noah's ark.
See Raja, the Bird Cage, the quaint little train—
You'll want to come back again and again!

Z

ARCHY's A-Z Fun Facts

A It would take winds greater than 150 mph to damage the Gateway Arch.

B There are no obstructed views in 50,222-seat Busch Stadium!

C CITY Museum was once the home of International Shoe Company, the world's largest shoe manufacturer.

D St. Louisans have been enjoying Ted Drewes's flavorful concoction since 1929.

E When the Eads Bridge opened on July 4, 1874, the parade was 14 miles long!

F Originally located at the Forest Park Highlands amusement park, the carousel, now at Faust Park, survived the 1963 fire that destroyed the Highlands.

G Built in 1855, Grant's Cabin is the only house still standing that was hand-built and occupied by U.S. president, Ulysses S. Grant. Grant's restored mansion, White Haven, is across the road from Grant's Farm.

H The Missouri History Museum's Jefferson Memorial stands on the site of the main entrance to the 1904 World's Fair.

I Two great sports museums in one place? It's true! The International Bowling Museum and Hall of Fame shares its home with the St. Louis Cardinals Hall of Fame Museum.

J Although its glass walls give the Jewel Box a delicate appearance, all of its horizontal surfaces are metal for the strength to weather hailstorms.

K Trains have been pulling into Kirkwood Depot since 1893!

L The lion has symbolized University City since 1909, when George Zolnay's sculptures were placed upon the pylons flanking Delmar Boulevard. Lion sculptures by William Baily adorn the entrance to University City's city hall, an octagonal building that once housed E.G. Lewis's publishing empire.

M The MUNY's revolving stage is reported to be the world's largest.

N The New Cathedral's mosaic is 83,000 square feet, the largest in the world!

O The dome on the Old Courthouse is 198 feet high and weighs 128 tons! The Old Courthouse has been the site of many landmark legal decisions, including the Dred Scott case.

P In the mid-1960s, Washington University students tied a big red bow around the McDonnell Planetarium as a holiday prank. St. Louisans loved the festive touch and have continued the tradition ever since!

Q Located in Queeny Park, The American Kennel Club Museum of the Dog features a "Guest Dog of the Week", including a live representative of the breed. Arf!

Fun
Facts

R By the early 1840s, St. Louis was a popular stop for tourists traveling by steamboat. Today people can still enjoy paddlewheel excursions from the St. Louis levee.

S In 1838, Julia Cerre Soulard gave the land on which Soulard Market now stands to the city of St. Louis, making Soulard Market the oldest public market west of the Mississippi.

T Turtle Park features several species of turtle found in Missouri—a snapping turtle, a Mississippi map turtle, a red-eared slider, three box turtles, and a stinkpot. More than 120,000 pounds of concrete were used to shape the 40-foot-snapping turtle!

U A whisper can be heard from one side of Union Station's 50-foot terminal arch to the other.

V Sumner High School in the Ville proudly claims among its alumni such famous St. Louisans as tennis great Arthur Ashe, rock'n'roll star Chuck Berry, comedian Dick Gregory, opera singer Grace Bumbry, TV anchorman Julius Hunter, and many others.

W One of the world's first skyscrapers, the Wainwright Building's design greatly influenced 20th-century urban architecture.

X·1 The St. Louis Walk of Fame features 95 bronze stars set in the sidewalk honoring St. Louisans who have made outstanding contributions to American culture. Each star is accompanied by a plaque summarizing the honoree's achievements.

X·2 The Saint Louis Art Museum is the only permanent building built for the 1904 World's Fair.

X·3 Born in England, Henry Shaw loved his adopted home of St. Louis and spared no personal expense to create the Missouri Botanical Garden. Opened to the public in 1859, the Garden enjoys international fame for its beauty and horticultural research.

X·4 Laumeier Sculpture Park is just one of two contemporary sculpture parks in the U.S. that has a museum. Laumeier also claims an outstanding international art collection, educational programs, and visiting exhibitions.

X·5 The Museum of Transportation boasts one of the nation's largest collections of railroad artifacts, including the world's heaviest steam locomotive, the 603-ton Union Pacific Big Boy.

X·6 Monk's Mound at Cahokia is the largest prehistoric earthwork in the Americas.

Y Lambert-St. Louis International Airport was once a balloon launch site called Kinloch Field. It was here that President Theodore Roosevelt, the first U.S. President to ride in an airplane, took his first ride.

Z The Bird Cage at the St. Louis Zoo was built by the Smithsonian Institution for the 1904 World's Fair. It is the largest outdoor bird cage in the world.

Fun Facts

© 2001 by Missouri Historical Society Press All Rights Reserved Published in the United States of America by Missouri Historical Society Press P.O. Box 11940, St. Louis, Missouri 63112-0040

Illustration copyright © 2001 Phyllis Harris Photography copyright © 2001 Gen Obata

05 04 03 02 01 5 4 3 2 1

Library of Congress Cataloging-in-Publication Data

Sandweiss, Lee Ann, St. Louis architecture for kids / by Lee Ann Sandweiss; illustrated by Phyllis Harris; photography by Gen Obata.

p. cm.

Summary: Introduces Saint Louis, Missouri, through rhymes about the city's architectural works and major attractions, presented alphabetically.
ISBN 1-883982-42-1 (alk. paper)

1.Architecture—Missouri—St. Louis—Juvenile literature. [1. Saint Louis (Mo.) 2. Architecture—Missouri—St. Louis. 3. Alphabet.] I. Harris, Phyllis, 1962— ill. II. Obata, Gen, ill. III. Title

NA735.S2 S27 2001
720'.9778'66-dc21   2001044397

Distributed by University of Missouri Press. Design by Phyllis Harris and Robyn Morgan. Cover photograph by Gen Obata.

Printed & bound in Canada by Friesens. Covers printed by Pinnacle Press, St. Louis, Mo.

Special thanks to the following individuals and organizations without whose enthusiasm and support this book would not have been possible:

Anheuser-Busch Companies, Inc., Bi-State Development Agency, Claire P. Budd, Katey Charles, Christy Childs, Doris Dana, Ted Drewes, Anna Goldbeck, Matthew Heidenry, William Iseminger, Jean Larson Steck, Nicola Longford, Barbara McNab, Robyn Morgan, Bev Pfeifer-Harms, Taylor Obata, St. Louis County Department of Parks and Recreation, The St. Louis Cardinals, The St. Louis Carousel at Faust Park, St. Louis Department of Parks, Recreation and Forestry, Eric Sandweiss, Carolyn Schmidt, Josh Stevens, Paul Wasielewski and Anabeth Weil.

Lee Ann Sandweiss would especially like to thank Dr. Robert Archibald and the Missouri Historical Society for the research leave that allowed her to work on this book.

Greater St. Louis

F   Faust Park

G   Grant's Farm

K   Kirkwood Train Station

Q   Queeny Park

X·4   Laumeier Sculpture Park

X·5   Museum of Transport

X·6   Cahokia Mounds

Y   Lambert-St. Louis International Airport